SCATTERSHOTS

a lighter verse
collection

Derek Kannemeyer

For Ele, and for Ed,

and for readers and writers of lighter verse everywhere.

TABLE OF CONTENTS

I. CBEASTS

I needed, I felt, a reset; a change of creative focus. So I compiled a list of 400 animals whose names began with the letter C. For a while I wrote only from this list—light verse, but also serious poems; plus song lyrics, short stories, even a short play. Stalking Crawlrollies, *inspired by Lewis Carroll's "The Hunting of the Snark," became a novel, half of it in nonsense verse form. The* CBeast *pieces selected for the present volume are narrower in genre, but I've tried to preserve some of the original tonal range. We'll begin with its second longest poem, the short story in rhyming couplets "Thalia and the Cockatoo."*

THALIA AND THE COCKATOO

I.
There dwelt, in Perth, Australia,
a cordially odd old stick named Thalia.
A life of comfort without color
had, by the decade, dimmed her duller,
and made her seem quite without vim—
but maybe that had all been *him*?
In widowhood, there came a change:
a *new* her woke; she woke up strange.
She pierced her ears for the first time;
bought ballgowns from the five and dime;
wore bedroom slippers to the store;
even knit mufflers for the poor.
She let her hair out, one might say—
what hair she had left, anyway—
spare cloud-grey clumps, that swirled untamed.
Her age? I do not know; she claimed:
"I'm 66, by Aussie stats,
since we live upside down, like bats!"
So, 99?—but since she told
that joke for years, let's stick with *old*.

II.
In her long life, her chief regret
was that she'd never owned a pet.
And so, before it got too late,
she strove to overcompensate.
She owned (at least! who could keep count
of all the kinds, and their amount?)
six snakes, three dogs, eleven cats,
seven white rabbits (five with hats),
eight mice, twelve fish (ten gold, two blue),
nine gerbils, and one cockatoo—

which she let loose about the house,
to hop and slink, to cat and mouse,
to gobble both it and each other.
She was a *laissez-faire* stepmother.
And every day she toured the show,
watching her family shrink and grow
and rut and feed and crap and shed
and bear new life, and drop down dead.
And all thought their menagerie
was home sweet home as home could be!
But there was one intrigued her more
than any other twenty-four:
the one like flame; the fire that flew
the bright, resplendent cockatoo.

III.
Thalia had led a sheltered life.
A parson's child, the gracious wife
of a wordless, frowning banker,
she'd played her role with meek, mild rancor.
(He died; she wept; some thought it grief;
some recognized it as relief.)
Free, still spry, childless, alone,
she neither envied anyone,
nor knew what else she ought to covet.
Her world seemed just the shape to love it.
The list of ordinary stuff
she didn't know was long enough
to sadden, shock, amuse, amaze,
and numb you all for days and days.
One example, here, will do;
it concerns the cockatoo.
She'd never learned that parrots speak;
that when one held them to one's cheek,

and crooned, "My darling," to such birds,
they might croon back those very words.
Our story is about to tell
of how she learned it, all too well.

IV.
Of all her pets, the cockatoo
stood out for vibrancy of hue:
a robe of red and yellow streaks;
a crown of spiky hot pink peaks.
She called him "Claude"—her husband's name,
she realized with a tinge of shame—
her mouth was used to it, that's all—
and Claude came swooping to her call.
He loved to nest in chandeliers,
as if to match his grace with theirs,
and when he rose, a dancing arc
of light pursued him through each dark
and cobwebbed corner of the room,
scrubbing her little world of gloom.
She used to set him on her finger,
and preen his throat so he would linger,
and when she cooed "My darling" to him,
she swore a tremble whispered through him.
If all Claude's language—then!—was *squawk,*
and *chirp, chirp, cheep* was all his talk,
yet oh, what heaven when he chirped!

All Hell broke loose the day he burped.

Thalia, who of course had taught him,
daily since the day she bought him,
how to shape and hold this note—
inadvertently, no doubt—

a minor gastric ailment—jerked.
She thought some belching burglar lurked.
She ducked; she screamed; the scream screamed back—
a dog barked, and awoke the pack—
soon, snarl for snarl, and growl for growl,
and mewl for mewl, and howl for howl,
the whole menagerie joined in,
each echoed by Claude's eerie twin.
A rabbit put in her two cents
and got four more in recompense;
the last of the surviving mice
squealed, and found it squealed back, twice;
a fly's buzz (bugs do crash the party)
became disquietingly hearty;
a snake of some kind's hooded hiss
doubled its esses, much like thisssssssss…
Even each fish's sploshy ripple
seemed there, in mid-air, to triple!
As swelling the scene's every crotchet,
and wheeling on wide wings to watch it,
there rose this Claude-of-all, this wonder,
this lightning dancing into thunder,
to rouse the rabble and whip it crackpot
till every two cents' worth hit jackpot.
What fun they had—all except Thalia,
who gasped, "My love has echolalia!"
Twisting in flight, Claude paused, and listened:
he'd heard her voice; his fierce eyes glistened;
"My darling," cooed the marvelous bird;
"Dear heart," he crooned; then barked; then purred;
and came to her to be caressed.
"My God!" cried Thalia. "He's possessed!"
As if by—no—she dared not say—
the man was dead—five years that day—

besides, the words the bird had said
had never entered that man's head!
"Dear heart," whispered Claude once more.
And Thalia swooned, and struck the floor.

V.
Oh Claude! If you could talk, how rash
to start with so outsized a splash.
Such wild news, unless broken gently,
unsettles certain hearers mentally…
When Thalia came to, she was bats.
She fed the last mouse to the cats;
she served a rabbit to the dogs,
garnished with junk-mail catalogs;
she placed two gerbils in a dish
and tried to feed them to the fish.
She chomped some this and that herself—
an old silk blouse, a plywood shelf,
seasoned with a little salt—
her dentures, luckily, called halt.
As for the demon bird, she chased
it round the house with cardboard paste,
but never got a decent swipe.
(She wasn't the athletic type.)
At length, by dint of perseverance—
despite some canine interference—
a sleeping pooch stretched out to fell her—
she trapped that parrot in the cellar.
Then sprawled against the door, and wept,
for words unsaid, and vows hard-kept;
for restless ghosts who would not die;
for sleeping dogs too long let lie;
for bold conclusions left unleapt to;
and when her grief was spent, she slept too.

VI.
In the cellar was a sink.
A tap's eye gave a slow, wet wink.
The dryer leaked a sock or two:
enough to feed a cockatoo.
All day, Claude scarcely made a sound.
He mapped the space out, flapped around
the walls, and gnawed the window locks;
slurped water from the tap; chewed socks;
but mostly, he listened at the door
to Thalia's soft, persistent snore.
When she began to wake, he purred
below the door a single word:
DARLING. He cooed it in her ear
in tones as tenderly sincere
as Thalia's own—for hers they were.
Lightly, he breathed them back to her,
a distant, intimate, slow sigh.
She grimaced, hard, but would not cry.
She swung the door. The cockatoo,
without a glance from her, flicked through,
bowed to a pooch, and gave one bark.
Thalia faced the cellar's dark.
"Claude," she said, "I know you're there.
It's time we talked." The musty air
rode up to her in earthy gusts.
She climbed down through a dance of dusts.
Some lights were out. One blazed, went dim,
and flickered dead: a sign? From him?

VII.
So what did poor, mad Thalia say
in that small underworld foray?

Was it the glittering ashes of
an old damped passion—was it love,
or tenderness—or else their lack—
she came to terms with in the black?
Did Claude the ghost—*can* ghosts?—respond,
unprompted, in a way more fond?
Neighbors, two weeks later, found
her stretched out on the bald stone ground,
almost comfortably dead,
his rain boots pillowing her head.
And that was the last they saw of her,
her buds and bairns in scales and fur:
her thirty cats, her forty rabbits,
indulging their dirty, naughty habits;
her hooded snake; the rodent hummock
bulging its slow way to its stomach;
her tranquil tank of fish, so still
they might perhaps be slightly ill;
her quivering, last-surviving gerbil;
her pooch; her pugs; even that verbal
magic show and cabaret,
that flying fireworks display,
that cockatoo she'd raised to hawk
back to her soul its own sweet talk.

VIII.
Oh, Thalia, what did you achieve,
conjuring such jokers from your sleeve?
Did it not seem rather late
to reinvent your simple fate?
To coddle pets, and name one "Claude,"
and as they chomped your house, applaud?
To limp down the dim cellar stair
to talk to ghosts not wholly there?

Oh, Thalia, if you hadn't blundered
you might have lived to be 100*—
a feat the whole world counts as stellar.
Instead of that, you chose the cellar—
too late to fix or greatly leaven
the hurt in you, or call it even,
for fifty years pent in his cage—
but not, perhaps, to *tell* your rage
to his and your own ghosts, who live
deep in the dark.
     Or to forgive?
To bare your heart's kept score of failure—
its griefs, its petty marginalia—
its silent spites, its secret shame—
and hear the dead avow the same?
Dear heart… Some blame, some guilt confessed,
grace granted, to be laid at rest,
snuggling his boots; poor dear old Thalia.

(* Or 001, in Perth, Australia.)

CONSIDERING THE COD

For my niece Ele, to whom I sent it in a birthday card when she was quite young. Decades later, she surprised me by reciting it back to me verbatim.

Consider the cod:
the oil of its liver,
which tastes very odd,
and makes my nose shiver,
and twists my mouth crooked,
and makes my face shudder
like someone just shook it,
is said by my mother
to do me great good—
it strengthens my blood—
or would if I took it.
(I find it less bother
to force-feed my brother.)

How hard on the cod
to have bile so nutritious!
How thoughtful of God
not to make it delicious.

LIFE & DEATH: THREE *CBEAST* MINIS

1. Dead Chimp Dis

With hard work, you could
Look darn near as good
As a dead chimpanzee.
Go ahead, primp and see!

2. Dead Carpet Beetle

Here lies a carpet beetle,
Squelched into a goo.
Don't weep and go all fetal:
You can't have your carpet and beetle too!

3. Live Chamois Shimmy

The chamois shimmies, lithe and svelte,
From crag to crag, to save his pelt.
It seems a shame to dust our desks
With what once danced such arabesques.
Instead of yelping, *Gimme, gimme!,*
I vote we let the chamois shimmy.

II. SCATTERSHOTS:
rhymes & rhythms random & twisted

Interlaced with the CBEASTS *(also with a selection of* LIMERICKS), *I'm placing a more general assortment of lighter verse pieces—starting with the sequence* FOLLIES & FOLDEROLS: *a hop and skip look at the history of light verse itself. It's a matter of some debate where the line falls between light verse and* real *poetry; some even argue that humor has no place in the latter—ceding to the former the richer, broader range! In dumb fun or smart fun, as sly wit or as blunt rage, in ways lightly song-like or wildly weird, long may its many, many styles of art be practiced!*

1. A Satire
satire: *"a poem in which wickedness or folly is censured"*
~Samuel Johnson

One of the oldest light verse styles is the satire, *a classical
mode favored in English by such wits as Alexander Pope
(1688-1744), in work ranging from the long mock-heroic
narrative poem "The Rape of the Lock" to the elegant two
line epigram:* I am his Highness's dog at Kew. // Pray tell
me, sir, whose dog are you? *Later satirists have at times
(as in my closing couplet) favored a coarser, blunter tone.*

You know those lines Pope had engraved
(what noble gifts he had, and gave!)
on the collar of the pet
he gave his Prince? A deft couplet
indeed, to satirize the sort
of toadies who frequent a court.

Had I a pug for Donald Trump,
I'd tattoo *Kiss here* on its rump.

2. A Cautionary Epigram
epigram: *a short witty poem; a literary device practiced for
over 2000 years; many satires are epigrams. Both terms
are now also routinely used in a broader, non-poetry sense.*

cautionary tale: *a moral tale, popular in folklore, to warn
against dangerous creatures, behaviors, and the like. The
satirist Hilaire Belloc (1870-1953) subverted the form in
nonsense verse tales whose characters come to sticky ends;
as in "Jim, Who Ran Away from his Nurse and was Eaten
by a Lion." I bow here to Belloc's ferocity of spirit.*

At the zoo, at their lair—dare we visit them there—
who'll blink? Who'll shrink at whose glare?
Who'll be the prey, who the lion, Hilaire?
Caveat lector, leo cave: of the satirist's eye, beware!

3. 'Twas on the Good Ship Polarity
*Epigrammatic wit has long been the province of literate,
sometimes very topical light verse. In the oral tradition,
comic verse is often of a bawdier and more basic nature.*

Here's to wit, and brevity—
the soul of wit! Refined
to tickle the quick mind.

And here's to that other levity—
dumb shtick to rock the belly
rude, crude, lewd, loud, smelly!

The kind, it may well be,
of more assured longevity,
as basic to our kind's
more base proclivities.

4. An Arrant Nonsense Poem

Light verse *in the more modern sense of the term has its roots in the 19th century. A major innovation was* nonsense poetry, *whose chief practitioners were English. Charles Dodgson (1832-1898), who published "The Hunting of the Snark," his Alice books, etc., as Lewis Carroll, lived from the age of 18 at the Oxford College of Christ Church. As a rule, residents were expected to be ordained as priests and take vows of celibacy. Dodgson acceded to neither rule, but evaded confrontation by remaining unmarried. A late 20th century tendency to label him a latent pedophile—on evidence that boils down to the "common sense" intuitions of a very different culture—still holds some popular sway. There is no evidence that he was an active pedophile.*

Charles Dodgson (aka Lewis Carroll)
made photographs, without their apparel,
of young girls, and charmed them with stories—
which (other times, other mores)
his contemporaries, the Victorians,
found sweetly admirable, say historians.
(Such pure little innocents, in their state of grace!
Still demurer, in a sense, without the strait lace.)

By contrast, the evidence of
Dodgson's quest for grown women to love—
he contrived the long visit, alone,
of free thinkers, without chaperone—
was suppressed by his family as shocking.
It would set the old wives' tongues to talking.

Yet in notions of sex, as primly reflex
as those we have mocked as too easily shocked,
we continue to tar Dodgson-Carroll's
two names, alas, with both barrels.

5. The Limerick: a mini-bio, in clerihew stanzas
limerick*: the form is folkloric, and before Edward Lear
(1812-1888) adapted and popularized it, it was raunchy,
exclusively male, and universally transgressive. ("Twas on
the good ship" is the start of a notoriously bawdy one.) It
has since evolved along both streams, the NSFW and the
more politely G or PG—though few follow Lear's model, of
mild-mannered nonsense verse with a first/last line refrain.*

clerihew: *a non-metrical four line poem, rhyming AABB, in
which the poet takes a humorous or oddball look at a real
biographical subject, who is named in the poem's first line.*

Edward Lear,
a peculiar, yet endearing old dear,
took the previously obscene limerick,
and taught it clean, primmer shtick.

"Derry Down Derry"—
how Victorian in what it finds merry!—
was the name he first published his under.
"And they survived this?!" we exclaim now in wonder.

Would "Mr. Abebika Kratoponoko Prizzikalo Kattefello
          Ablegorabalus Ableborinto Phashyph"
(Lear's favorite alias) have found his book dumped in
          the trash if
Lear had gone instead with *that* pseudonym?
But he didn't. Well, good on him.

6. The Bentleys: a family tree in three light verse forms
clerihew: *a light verse form invented and popularized by
Edmund Clerihew Bentley (1875-1956). He generally
published (novels, journalism) as E.C. Bentley, but as a
humorist he preferred E. Clerihew Bentley.*

(a) *This is a Clerihew*
E. C. B.'s grandfather Alfie
owned spinning mills and was wealthy.
John Edmund Bentley, his dad,
played rugby for England. Not bad!

(b) *This is a Limerick*
E. C., though financially healthy,
perhaps had more bats in his belfry.
His first claim to fame
is a verse form, whose name,
"clerihew," is kind of a selfie.

(c) *This is a Double Dactyl*
Devilish-cleverly,
Clerihew Bentley
also wrote mysteries—
like *Trent's Last Case*—

a Golden Age classic which
semi-impenetrably
pelts its detective
with egg in the face.

(d) *This is a Second Clerihew*
Clerihew's son, Nicolas Bentley,
after quitting school to be a circus clown, incidentally,
was the illustrator for T.S. Eliot's *Old Possum*—
which strikes me as awesome!

(e) *This is a Second Double Dactyl*
Chockablock poppycock,
Nicolas Bentley
also did Belloc's *New
Cautionary Tales*

Talk about Golden Age!
Casuistically,
Hilaire's hilarious!
(Eliot pales.)

7. Beware Hilaire: a Bonus Cautionary Limerick
*Hilaire Belloc ostensibly wrote for children. Since him,
children's literature is as likely to be tart as it is sweet.*

Beware! It's Hilaire! His stuff's scary—
or funny—opinions do vary!
You may wish to quarrel,
likewise, with his moral.
Is it what it is, kids? Be wary!

8. A Brief Ode to the Most Prolific and Versatile Anon
*You who live while I lie dead how did you make this song?
We told his rhyme to her and they remembered it all wrong.*

Anon!
You sine qua non!
You star, you!
(I'm sorry. Who *are* you?)

9. The Double Dactyl: a meditation, in limerick stanzas
*double dactyl: a metrically exact two quatrain verse form
invented by Anthony Hecht and Paul Pascal; popularized
by Hecht and John Hollander. Line 1 is nonsense jangle,
line 2 names the poem's subject, line 6 is one long word,
and lines 4 and 8 rhyme. (E.g. as in my sections 6c and 6e).
Hecht (1923-2004), a master formalist, was in his serious
mode one of America's finest 20th century poets. Also a
master formalist was Mr. Hollander (1929-2013), whose
profoundly witty book on poetic forms,* Rhyme's Reason, *I
checked out and renewed so often that when a new edition
came out the librarian gave me the old copy to keep.*

For his new form (created—I checked—
with Paul Pascal) Anthony Hecht
provided strict rules—
a workbench of tools,
to shape one. Some leave that room wrecked.

Apologies, Pascal and Hecht, if
adherence grows blithely selective—
"Begin with a dollop
of jolly codswallop"—
it's a double-dactylic directive!

But forms, when they're well-loved, evolve.
To start lightly fresh. Or revolve,
in like fall and lift,
about centers that shift.
To surprise us in how they resolve.

To break bad, and breed in the rift.

10. An Interpolation: World Studies

A word, as we crisscross the pond,
about the larger world beyond:
I know my history-flit's parochial;
that other tongues can frame a joke, y'all!
J'adore, say, the surrealist
Robert Desnos: so French a twist!
I love, *auf Deutsch*, the quirky turn
taken by Christian Morgenstern.
By luck, I read those two in school!
But who's the big fish in *your* pool?
Tell me your must-reads, people! Thanks!
Back to mine now, though. Two Yanks.

11. Dorothy & Ogden: a temperamental yin & yang

(a) *For Dorothy Parker (1893-1967)*
Dorothy Parker
was fond of the caustic remark. Her
wit, off the cuff as in verse,
was quick; and dismissive; and terse.

Was an eye ever sharper and darker?
Or a tongue, for better or worse?
Or a temperament? Dorothy Parker
found Dorothy Parker's a curse.

(b) *For Ogden Nash (1902-1971)*
Ogden Nash
talked way less trash.
The fun he fried up
came sunny side up.

12. Across the Subverse: a double double dactyl
Theodore Seuss Geisel (1904-1991), writing as Dr. Seuss,
strove to make the messages in his illustrated children's
tales not too overt. Children can see that coming, he said.
His aim, he claimed, was to be more "subversive."

Op ed cartoonist
Theodore Geisel
raged against fascists,
racists, and such.

His stories for children,
Bippo-No-Bungusly,
work the same ground
with a whimsical touch.

The places we go
down the Hoober-Bloob Highway!
Its words wink like baubles!
Kids giggle, kids clutch!

Till Yertl the Turtle asks,
Humpf-Humpf-a-Dumpferly,
Do your *ville and* Hoo*ville*
differ *that much?*

13. For Stephen Sondheim: a Theater Nerd's Salute
Throughout history, a lot of the wittiest writing in verse
was done for the stage. It still is, in the very collaborative
field of musical theater. From that world let me pick out
Stephen Sondheim (1930-2021) to gush in song about.

How fond I'm
Of Sondheim!—
Whose merit lies in and beyond rhyme—
In seeing, and telling, in song—
But whose art and its tender asperities
Depend on the hands-on dexterities
Of staging, to go right or wrong.
And then, oh, man, there it is: sublime all along!
In what kind of pantheon do he and his kind not belong?

14. Envoi: Further Reading
Here's a toast to a few other favorites:

To Wodehouse: so charming! And Dahl, more alarming.
Silverstein, ickier. Cope, Stallings, pickier.
Swift, all disgust and harangue.
And Gilbert, and Porter, and Brassens, and Lehrer—
the lyricist wits of each land and era
who have penned whip-smart verse the world sang!

All praise their yin, and their yang—
the range, the shebang of those best of us!
With a clap on the back for the rest of us:
who may not have much more than the zest of us
to deem ourselves part of their gang.

I have a little list.
But you'd all of you be missed.

CORGIS AND BESS

A different response to Pope's couplet; this time a CBeast *poem. The number of the Queen's corgis fluctuated: there are photos of her with seven; the peak is thought to have been nine. After young adulthood, only from 2018-20 was she without one. One, Susan, accompanied her on her honeymoon. In 2015 she stopped breeding corgis, not wishing her pups to suffer the abandonment of her death. During the COVID-19 lockdown, however, with Prince Phillip ill, she was given new dogs to help her through.*

I
We were the famed Welsh herding dogs,
bred small and lithe for crags and bogs.

As tough as Jeeps, we held in line
loud, scrawny herds of sheep and swine.

Those hard hills, that ancestral seat
are old boasts here on Easy Street,

where we are the royal seven-pack.
The Queen is our shepherd. We shall not lack.

II
We are Her Majesty's dogs at Buckingham.
We check the stables. Grooms are mucking 'em.

About the palace grounds we go,
our tails aloft, our noses low,

to map the smells and smooch the trails;
our noses low; aloft our tails.

III

We are Her Majesty's dogs at Windsor.
No tours today: the *Queen* is in, sir!

We sniff the trees; our watery mark
striates the royal woodland bark.

IV

We are Her Majesty's dogs at Blenheim.
She's visiting. She's dressed in denim.

We frolic in the grass, and claim
these gardens in her royal name,

as the dogs of Her Majesty's subjects dance
their growling, cowed obeisance.

V

We are Her Majesty's dogs; we pass
from here to there behind plate glass.

The Rolls Royce smell succumbs to ours.
Our sevenfold odor overpowers

the musked bouquet of bottled fogs:
for we are hers, Her Majesty's dogs.

Sometimes, dogs bark along the way.
Our ears prick up: whose dogs are they?

As we sound our gruff repertoire
of howls—to answer who *we* are—

she'll wave, sometimes—as though to bless
that dimly swarming emptiness—

but rarely glances out; the crowds
that line the streets waft by like clouds—

waft greyly by, like long-banked rain.
We watch them, through the plate glass pane.

VI

We are Her Majesty's private solace:
her butt of sack; her whist; her Wallis.

Her public face is looked at hard.
Though she was bred for such regard,

it takes her impassioned breath to steer
these squabbling herds from there to here,

across this bald and worked-out land,
through weather deaf to her command.

Her public life consuming her,
her private hands caress our fur.

She does her duty, as ever we did,
who lick her royal nose as needed;

and ring her round, to bring like sheep
her stray dreams home, in snuffled sleep.

TWO COBRA PIECES
*The second of these is reprinted (in reworked form) from
my browsing book of animal factoids and light verse
quatrains called* A Betabestiary. *Go check it out!*

1. Cobra Dance

A watchful cobra rears and sways,
en garde against an Indian flute.
How svelte his dance: the music plays
what seems a cordial salute.

In fact, the snake is poised to strike;
the flute's a kind of prodding stick.
One stands in formal, tall dislike;
the other turns a business trick.

And yet how gracefully the pair,
in counterpoise made sinuous,
conduct their ritual affair—
seducing, not themselves, but us.

2. Dangerous Liaisons

Petting your Cobra gets them frisky.
Beware! And keep yours off the whisky!
If he were drunk, or I were soberer,
I might not greatly trust my Cobra.

III. LIMERICKS

There's one form I work in (or play in) so often that my selections need their own section of this book: limericks! The earliest known limerick—in form, at least—is apparently a 13th century Latin prayer, by Thomas Aquinas. But in English it derives from an early 18th century Irish drinking song, with bawdy stanzas and a singalong refrain—one variant of which included the line "Won't you come up to Limerick?" (I apologize to lovers of work at that end of the spectrum: mildly risqué is as far as I'm prepared to go.) The form wasn't called a limerick— Lear never used the name—until the late 19th century.

PTO for my limerick mock ars poetica.

THE ART OF THE LIMERICK

Its darts should be light. But well-placed
to effect some assault on good taste.
Just to tickle, or pinch—
not so much that we flinch—
only groan, and feel slyly unchaste.

"There are photos (that I won't attach)
of my wife naked, lifting a match.
In her favorite of me,
I am clothed, sipping tea,
and could pass for a dopey sasquatch."

See how delicate? Like a soufflé!
It would fall flat, were I to say, say,
"nude with a cactus."
You'd think, "Ouch!" (The fact is
she *was*, though. And things went okay.)

YOUR CACHALOT
"Cachalot" is another word for the sperm whale.

I.

Feed squid to your cachalot—
And make it a real spread—
When he grooms your moustache a lot,
He's feeling underfed.

II.

If he's sneezing ash a lot
(His blowhole's in his snout)
He may be smoking hash a lot.
He needs to cut that out!

III.

Be careful, though! It's rash (a lot)
To bash him with a stick,
Or crowd him, talking trash a lot:
Remember Moby-Dick?

COELACANTH, JANUARY 1939

*A species of crossopterygian ganoid fish, thought to be
extinct since the cretaceous period, until a five foot long,
127 pound specimen was caught off the Cape Province,
South Africa coast in December 1938. I was born in Cape
Province, which may be why this tale, for me, has acquired
an extra layer of romance.*

Old Coelacanth is most discreet—
you hardly ever know he's there.
Perhaps because he has no feet,
he leaves no footprints anywhere;
nor ever sits (he has no seat)
to ride the sea's great rocking chair.

When dinosaurs were frisky things,
before the first whale learned to swim
or dolphins spread their lack of wings,
crossopterygians like him,
no hands, in hordes, like playground kings,
clambered the sea's great jungle gym.

A leopard cannot change its spots,
but sly old Coelacanth's a fish:
he spawned amphibious tiny tots,
who shifted with a stippled swish.
They took shore leave; let down their fur.
Old dad kept mum; lay low with her.

For more than 70 million years
his self-effacement was colossal.
Now off our bow he reappears—
where living sea-beasts swarm and jostle—
still wet behind his lack of ears—
who last month was an ancient fossil.

Last month's cognoscenti said,
of his whole hairless, hidden breed,
nor hide nor hair still haunts the bed
he took to then, dark ages past—
before a dream of Adam's seed
brought light unto the void at last.

Just one crossopterygian,
they say, survives now: only he
in all the vast and Stygian
discretion of the teeming sea.
The world is rich with asterisks.
Here, in our net, one flaps and frisks.

FOODSTUFF & NONSENSE

A Scattershots *sequence—but beginning with a CBeast, and featuring a* limerick. *One reason I intersperse rather than separate the sections is that they overlap.*

1. Table Benediction: To a Crab

O Crab,
Who we're faster than we grab:
Your claw
Was the arm, once, of that law.

But take heed:
Who we're slower than we feed.
Your life
Is at the sharp end of this knife.

2. Blood Sausage

One of the grosser groceries—
its squish, its color—*so* cerise—
even its smell—sniff closer!—is
blood sausage!

It's made of cooked blood. No, not yours!
A cow's, a sheep's, a pig's, a boar's—
stuffed in a casing. (Are those pores?
Yucckkk, blood sausage!)

I don't know much about the taste.
I choose to back away in haste.
But let's not let it go to waste!
Here! Some blood sausage?

3. Cool as a Cucumber?

Cucumbers aren't cool! In fact,
as a rule, they're gruesome.
On dates, they don't know how to act.
They slurp. They drool. Their noses run.
They read their lines from cuke cards stacked
beside their plate. They call you *hon*.
And do they *pay*? Ask anyone
who ever grew or wooed some!

They dance, but cukes are cumbersome.
They prance, and juke, but lumber some—
best not risk a twosome.

A few may golf—or go to shows,
and hum, off-key, the numbers some—
or bum loose change—say *No!* to those.
But most prefer to slumber some,
snoring until you goose 'em.

Since juiced cukes make a trendy drink,
it might seem cool to juice 'em.
Beware of what the cool folks think!
Always, first ask, "Where's the sink?"
should someone offer *you* some.

4. The Earl of Sandwich

Because the Earl's workload would scupper
his plans, sometimes, for a cooked supper,
he invented the sandwich!
(His staff lent a hand. Which
is why only half the crust's upper.)

5. Feud over the Lack of Ham in a Ham Sandwich

"That little bit's a bit too little!"
cried the customer, annoyed.
"I was not a little nettled
to find I bit upon a void!"

The server, not a bit unsettled—
the snarky little shit enjoyed
seeing folks hiss and sputter spittle
like an old adenoidal kettle—

surveyed the plate, scoffed in rebuttal,
"A bit late now, now you've destroyed
every jot and bit of tittle
of the evidentiary victual—

it's bitten to bits of who knows *what* all."
"This restaurant I will avoid!"
returned the customer. "Regret'll
be your lot, and not a little!"

And bitterly his belt he buckled,
chin he blotted of its spittle,
bile he strained (in vain) to bottle,
bill he (tip remittal) settled,

and still more than a little nettled—
fuming like Popocatépetl—
oh, for somebody to throttle!—
stormed out, what a lot annoyed.

TWO CHRISTMAS CAROLS

1. *Caribou Carol*
The caribou, watching this night
the flickering, prancing flight of their otherworldly kin,
high where the stars wink out and in above the tundra,
imagine they too can fly.

Tossing off ice-spars with an antlered swish, they lift
their broad hoofs up through permafrost; they lock
thrust horns with gravity. Great gust-gifts
of their unribboning breath exchange to sky—
their shoulders brace and shove—until a lost, rocked,

startled-into-wonder world breaks under
the weight and spin of them into ice-hiss
and dusk glitter; and the musk of this
Christmas night into flocked caribou; into sung thunder.

2. *Angels Blessing*
With star-strung wings and moons for faces,
with crescent mouths, and wide, round eyes,
may angels bless your inner spaces—
blue-whale your seas, bird-cry your skies—
paddling in white isosceles
gowns that swish to show their knees
the fluffy, fleecy, floccus breeze.

By all most sacred—which is breath,
pulsing strong, and sweet, and sharp,
I repeat this shibboleth:
may we banjo as we harp.
There's not much creepier, I think,
than wide, round eyes that do not blink.
Let ours be fonder, child: to watch, but wink.

ELSIE IN ETHERLAND

*My favorite light verse poet? Incontrovertibly—unless
Vikram Seth's novel in verse* The Golden Gate *counts—it's
Lewis Carroll. In an early version, the protagonist of this
next piece was Carroll's Alice. There remain traces of her.*

1.
The next step Elsie took,
the pages of her book
riffed her to a summer
wood. Light breezes shook
a sunlit dapple from a
poplar by a brook.
She entered there, to look,
where shadows mouthed and mimed.

She chose a tree. She climbed.
The sun cast its gold light.
This limb with that limb rhymed!
She laughed, and climbed some more,
as leaves jigged with delight,
up into the ether's ore,
to perch in that highest crook
where dares dangle their hook—
or what are stories for?

The crown was thick with berries—
some sweet, some tart, like cherries—
so Elsie chugged a few—
and light as a leaf she grew!
How sweetly the wind blew,
lifting the leaves aloft—
oh, it tugged at Elsie too!
She laughed, and rode its waft
to where the eagles flew.

And there—finding, unplanned,
more berries in her hand—
she laughed, and chugged the lot!
And as if seized by her collar,
and hurled there, with its holler,
beyond the moon she shot!
How, thought Elsie, *grand!*
The earth and all its squalor
shrank to a tiny dot.

2.
"Gates Crew!" an angel cried,
flurrying to her side
upon a drift of cloud.
His sign said "Joy Tours Ride."
"No photographs allowed,
but nice of you to visit.
I'm Peter. Alice, is it?
Hop on! The view's exquisite."

They strolled the upper deck.
"Wow, what the actual heck,
Saint Petey!" Elsie gushed.
Saint Peter smiled and flushed.
"I helped," he said. There were
cliff tops—"See there?"—of myrrh
he'd fringed with conifer.
"Well, *supervised*!" He blushed.

"Wow! Wow!" she said, as if
she'd figured out *which* cliff.
"Here," he said, "take a pew!"
She sat. They spoke together,
politely, about the weather,
for a courteous minute or two,
the way well-bred folk do,
when meeting someone new.

Conditions, it seemed, were always
(apart from in the hallways,
where drafts got in) divine!
Each day, so crisp, so fine,
like Earth's best spring and fall days—
and yet *uniquely* so—
just as with flakes of snow—
in Elsie's world below!

Alas, no, there weren't *seasons*
in Heaven! Why? Who could say?
But God must have His reasons.
(*Or His "mysterious way."*
Pete blushed, and spoke no treasons.)
Elsie must ask one day
when she returned to stay!
So *might* she return…? "You may!"

But there ended the tour.
He winked, and said no more—
just clinked her mug of tea,
and gave a last small pour
to toast the Trinity—
as with each sip she drank,
the sky beneath her shrank,
until she awoke, as me.

ELBOW ODE
for Sara

I.
We're guys.
We fetishize
bare flesh. A shoulder,
exposed, can make us smolder.

I knew
a woman who
snorted, "If our clothes
bared nothing but elbows,

men, since men are toads,
would pen us elbow odes."
I read her one to knees.
"Oh, yuck," she said. "Oh please."

II.
Flesh needn't be all bare
to draw the hungry stare.
A lacy sleeve or two
would very likely do

to make us gulp, and reel,
and wish to cop a feel.
"Oh, yuck," my buddy squalls.
"I'd elbow you in the balls."

III.
We're on a plane. Not much
elbow room. Ours touch.
She's cute. There may be sparks.
"There aren't," she remarks.

CAT, CAT: for Buckwheat

Cat, cat,
Our house acrobat—
Who leaps to my stomach—to paw, and to pat—
   to plump up a tuft, and to smooth it back flat—
   to pause and to pose on my summit of fat,
   as if I'm where it's at!—
And you find contentment in that!

Cat, cat, cat—
You furball, you purr-doll, you captor of hats—
You noser of knickknacks, you snatcher at gnats—
You nap-catcher, lap-lounger, peeker through slats—
You nudger of shadows that shift on the mat,
   as if there's contentment in that!

Cat! Cat! Cat!
For lack of a rat,
   must you pick on that vole to corner and bat?
Why leap on some songbird and squish the thing flat?
Oh, the games you play with my heart's thermostat—
   as if finding contentment in that!

Oh, cats, cats, cats, cats, cats—
Since the very first cats your cat Adam begat,
   and the litters of kittens of all of *those* cats—
   in ziggurats, laundromats, mansions and flats—
   from skittish cat pipsqueaks to brash fat cat brats—
We've had cats come find us, to sit where we're sat—
   to smooch, and to snuggle, to scratch, to chitchat,
   with meows, or with trills, or squealed caveats—
Who have yowled us awake just to get belly pats—
   and pushed things off tables to watch them go splat!
Who have poked us, and clawed at us, driven us bats—
And we've found contentment in that.

THREE LIMERICKS

1. Bond Flick

We gasp/flinch/guffaw at the blunderings
of the smug villain's stooges and underlings.
And we cheer—Bond's so cool!
See those hot Bond babes drool!
See that ice bitch flash her killer underthings!

2. Crime Boss

A Kremlin spy-mobster called Putin
could not find a suit to look cute in—
but at least he was ripped,
so he walked around stripped,
in combat boots, putting the boot in.

3. Nascarpet

A young Nascar fan from Vancouver
liked practicing with an old Hoover.
What loud, lovely noise
as he crashed through his toys!
Just the way to make vroom to maneuver!

NINE LIVES: SELECTIONS FROM THE TALES OF PRETTY POLYGLOT

1. Or, The Caged Bird of Limerick, Who, Remembering
Her Past Lives, Spoke Tajik & Slavic & Cymric—&
Gothic & Punic, Italic & Runic—Coptic & (So She
Claimed) Turmeric; & In Rhyming Form Told Of Them

She had fleas, and her tail-plumes hung tattered,
but she rocked on her perch and she chattered,
in Maori, and Danish,
both flowery and plainish,
till none of that other stuff mattered.

Astonishing! How could a bird who
lived locked in a cage, pooping bird do,
chirp, prattle, and squawk
in Welsh and Mohawk?
Talk Thai, and Rumanian, and Urdu?

There are tales told, by the old wives,
where after death, memory survives—
some say with this bird
some such thing occurred—
and that mostly, she spoke of past lives—

oh, I doubt it! But not much else jives.

2. A Cassowary, New Guinea

When I was a wild Cassowary
I rarely ate doughnuts, or dairy.
Fresh fruit was my fave!
Though sometimes I'd crave
fish, frogs, or fronds. It would vary.

When I was a wild Cassowary,
I was quiet, and quite solitary.
I lived in the forest—
but came as a tourist
sometimes to the palm scrub or prairie.

When I was a wild Cassowary
I was not so much shy: I was wary.
I had claws, I was big,
with a helmet-hard wig,
but the world was big too. Which was scary.

The life of a wild Cassowary
is no more or less ordinary
than anyone's is—
than hers, theirs, yours, his—
Well, maybe a little. But barely.

3. A Camel, Camelot

Oh, that life as a Camel—in Camelot!
Their learned men called me a sham a lot.
"It claims that it came here from Mesopotamia,
wherever *that* is. Says it swam a lot!"
They laughed at me, mostly, in Camelot.

My friend Jonah lived in a Cachalot.
Those know-it-alls called that tale trash a lot.
They'd swig mead from flagons and boast of the dragons
they'd almost slain, once, and say "Damn!" a lot.
Pinch the barmaids, and jingle their cash a lot.

I had one true champion: Sir Lancelot.
We voyaged together through France a lot.
What tall tales he spun of the kind I was one of!
What romances to charm the *belles dames* a lot!
How they'd lean on his shoulder and dance a lot!

I went for long walks by the wharf a lot.
The sailors, a lewd and unlawful lot,
declared me their mascot: some raced me at Ascot;
some ran rum, and slipped me a dram a lot.
One fixed me up dates with a dwarf a lot.

I was never an Ox, or an Ocelot.
I can't say I've felt that a loss a lot.
What lot mine was *not* counts a lot less than what
I *was* once: a Camel from Camelot.
As lots go, that wasn't an awful lot.

4-7. Brief Lives

Crow, Crozet, VA
When I was a Crow from Crozet, I used a crowbar to
crochet. My style was chromatic, and so acrobatic I
could crochet while playing croquet.

Cheetah, Cheatham, TN
I once was a Cheetah in Cheatham. I chased
Tenneseeans to eat 'em. By the flicker of stars,
through circus cage bars, as the licking moon lit my
tapetum.

Caiman, Grand Cayman
One time, as a Caiman, named Eamonn, I chomped the
left leg off a shaman. Left maimed by a caiman he'd
claimed tamed, that shaman became, shamed, a layman.
(A lame un.)

Cygnet, Swansea, Wales
I once was a Cygnet from Swansea. My parents were
white; I was bronzy. My white father took his white pen,
and they wrote me—this mystery—then: white father,
white mother, brown daughter; this signature, trailed in
brown water.

8. Noah's Carp

I was one of the ark carp—carpooling
On a magical carpet—unmuddied,
As the black sky caved in like tarpaulin,
And Karpinsk to Carpathia flooded.
Imagine the frisson of seeing
Earth, sea, sky, fused in one freshet.
My fins itched to carpe that diem!
To divebomb that salt skirl and thresh it!
          And sing hey, ho, the wind and the water!

But for months we stayed cooped in our carpark—
Maybe three million couples and Noah—
Where the zebu lay down with the aardvark,
And the sasquatch squeezed in with the boa.
And for months, as escarpments of sea rose
Outside our small freshwater porthole,
We watched our salt cousins—such heroes!—
Scale wild bucking whitecaps and chortle,
          With a hey, ho, the wind and the water!

Oh, I don't mean to carp, but when, later,
Waves trailing their lace skirts down Ararat,
I tobogganed a fall of spring water
To this lake, with a wet-through Sahara rat,
I'd have wagered the soul of my species
On a prayer to adapt, and the notion
Desire's the perdition it preaches,
To have drowned for one hour in that ocean—
          Singing hey, ho, the wind and the water!

9. A Siamese Fighting Cock, Bangkok

When I was The Cock from Bangkok.
I brawled, and humped hens, and drank hock.
I mauled till they wept.
I crowed till I slept.
Told the farmer to get a dang clock.

I was Cock of the Walk. There were Chicks
who would mail me tail-feathers for kicks.
From Bombay to Bangkok,
my face and John Hancock
made them dance in their dreams and do tricks.

I had plumes. I had claws. I had legs.
I had moves. I had babes. They had eggs.
Had I brains? I had none.
Had I taste? I had *fun*.
And I drained that malt corn to the dregs.

Did I live cock-a-hoop till I died?
Did I age fast, punch-drunk and cock-eyed?
Was I cooked? Was I through?
I was too tough to chew,
and I smashed Satan's teeth when he tried.

Who could ever be pleasure's slave,
and cockscombed with heat, and not crave
to be King of that Rut?
I held sway. I had strut.
And I leaned on them hard till they gave.

TWO TRIOLETS

1. Cottontail Triolet

Cottontail, turn tail and run,
a streak of brown, and grey, and gone.
The horned owl comes, who culled your son.
Cottontail, turn tail now—run—
live to birth a quicker one.
The grey fox loiters, looking on—
cottontail, turn tail and run—
a streak, of brown, and grey, and gone.

2. Time Triolet

"Darling, mine, let's steal an hour
from our impossibly tight schedule,
to sit a while—just to devour—"
"We can do that? Us? An hour?"
"more of our book! To let its power—"
"I wish, my darling! But you *said* you'll—"
"And I will, darling! In, let's say, an hour?"
" I wish, darling! But my love, the schedule?"

COUGAR, COUGAR

Cougar, cougar, muscled sprawl
of mountain sand made animal:

stretched upon a ledge, you doze
in sunlit animal repose,
the pictograph, in claw and fur,
of vanishing America.

And dream of ranging through the dark,
your hierogram this graceful arc
that claws shut on a throat of deer,
and snarls your name into her ear:

cougar, cougar, muscled sprawl
of mountain sand made animal.

A COW

A cow isn't easy to flummox.
Do we think on our feet?
Do we sleep on our stomachs?
A cow is less easy to flummox;
she thinks with her stomachs;
she sleeps on her feet.

She ponders the cosmos and chews.
Every so often, she moos.
Asleep on her feet, does she dream of her stomachs—
abomasum, omasum, reticulum, rumen—
the halls of consumption, inhuman and human?
The eating and eaten, the being replete?
Or is she dreaming of woodlands and hummocks;
of pools where the dragonflies play;
of plains where the gnu and the buffalo run,
her lean country cousins, grazed under the gun?
As the dusk turns to night, and the dawn turns to day,
and she ruminates once, and she ruminates twice,
and she chews on her cud in the prairie.
Might it have been safer, if maybe less nice,
to work from a stall at the dairy?
But she likes it out here where it's airy—
where the stars pierce the dark and illuminate
the gloom in which ruminants ruminate—
just to ponder the cosmos, and moo,
as cows do, as they chew, and they chew.

We may think on our feet,
we may sleep on our stomachs,
but a cow is less easy to flummox.
She thinks with her stomachs.
She sleeps on her feet.

THREE LIMERICKS

1. Finger Food

A bulimic nailbiter named Claire
having bitten her fingertips bare
kept nibbling on
till her knuckles were gone
and she threw up both hands in despair.

2. The Voice

A high windows washer from Fiji
had put too much soap on his squeegee.
He, *whoosh,* hit a bush,
crotch first, and then smoosh!
And now he can sing like a Bee Gee!

3. Spiritual Dilemma

"I think the earth's doomed, dad," sighs Jesus.
"Pollution, war, global diseases.
Should *we* un-debacle it?
Or watch, and eat chocolate?"
"Let's watch," says God. "See if hell freezes."

CANARY IN THE COAL

Life is cheap, cheeps Canary,
        and the hard black coal burns fair.
The soot-throat men and I are gathering
        fistfuls of black fire.

Seven thin skeins of moonlight
        swing from the crawling lamps.
I ride shotgun through bouncing shadows;
        the roof's dark shoulder slumps.

My black man's hollowed me a nest
        of finely knotted wire.
He sets me in the glittering dirt
        to sip the skimpy air.

And he smashes echoes from the wall,
        in dense, dust-skittering clumps;
my chest's a gold sock in black boots;
        my throat's a dark green glimpse.

Before I was the black man's pet,
        such greens and golds were all my truth.
This face smiled open at the seams.
        We jumped down King Coal's mouth.

Now when I die (cries Canary)
        I hope my black man's there,
to scoop me from my nest, into
        the tangles of his hair,

and dream with him of fruit trees,
        and the sun's great golden tooth—
beside blue lakes, where slim white winds
        catch and shift their breath.

Life is cheap (chirps Canary),
          and the hard black coal comes dear.
The soot-throat men are gathering
          fistfuls of black fire.

MY COCKATIEL AND THE CARDINALS

My cockatiel's a quiet thing
who sits unblinking in her cage,

and saves her strength for dieting
on small, cracked husks of something beige.

She's mostly grey and white and black—
a kind of gaunt, ascetic pigeon—

but on each cheek, an orange smack
recalls a gaudier religion,

while at the crown, punk-yellow curls
flex in an imagined breeze.

Outside her window, great red swirls
of cardinals bedeck the trees.

LITTLE CRITTERS

Sometimes, when fits of jitters hit,
you've been where little critters sit.
Sometimes they bite a bit and flit;
sometimes they stay, stake out a patch,
and make out, mating where you scratch.
You're where the *new* lice like to hatch!—
    twice as hungry; thrice as small!
    You might not find it nice at all.

Sometimes, we may just shift, and twitch,
and scratch the bit they bit, and bitch.
Sometimes, every inch an itch,
we pinch and flinch till which is which?
Although I hate to criticize
some itty-bitty critter's size,
    I do not think it fair at all
    to be so hardly there at all.

I try to live each day with relish.
I sniff each rose. I snub what's hellish.
Should big, bad, beastly creatures loom,
I rise, and bow, and leave the room.
But how to blithely carpe diem
when seized by jaws too small to see 'em?
    I do not think it or cute, or sweet,
    to be so brutally petite.

While lions, sharks, might like, perhaps,
to maul me into smaller scraps,
none ever has! Yet some wee critter
can feed, then breed, then tell its litter
I'm their brunch—and babysitter?
    I'd find it far more bearable
    if they—or I—weren't there at all.

CENTIPEDES

Centipedes are earnest creatures
with small, slow brains and homely features:
a creepy, crawly cord of skeins;
a nervous lack of bones and veins.
Their name means "hundred feet"—and they
can only hope they're who they say.
It worries them, as well it may.
Settling on some basement shelf
to take their inventory of self,
they sift through dust, and try to keep
a running count, but fall asleep.
They've souls of stockroom clerks, perhaps,
but still they're honest, earnest chaps.

In the evening, when they rise,
they wash their face, uncross their eyes,
and count their feet to make quite sure
they've neither shed nor grown one more.
They'd feel obliged to change their name,
should once the count not prove the same...
It does! It does! It does! And yet—
Still they doubt, and still they fret:
the proof's so pat; the math so neat.
Let X denote the sum complete...
Then what (they count it, on their feet)
it comes to must be...? X, perhaps?
The souls of clerks, but honest chaps.

It's hard to not know where one stands.
If they, like us, could have two hands
to count on, could it be that they,
like us, might know they're who they say?

TWO POLITICAL DAMP SQUIBS

*#1 first appeared in 2021, in the journal "Rigorous," as
"Because He Just Won't Go Away." But he continued not
to, so I changed the title to "A November Prayer." But that
prayer wasn't answered. And #2 proved just as ineffectual.*

1.
Divest him of everything that is bluster:
of the proofs he trumpets without naming;
of the beautiful plans he promises and can't muster;

denude him of the sycophants who swell
the echo chamber of his sneers, and of his blaming,
tolling his tocsins as their temple bell.

Unvarnish his every lie, Lord, of its Big Man luster—
to double talk, doubled down on—the hard sell
of nothing multiplied by nothing, which is nothing—

scrub his every orifice of the murderous whiny
insinuations with which he fans his minions' loathing—
until lo! Stripped of the smoke blowing from his heinie,

the man who would be emperor has no clothing;
and behold, his wiener is tiny.

2.
"Barack *Hussein* Obama,"
sneers Don *Who's Insane* Trump.
What's in a name? "Yo mama!"
to Donald on the stump.

His middle name's American,
So he's no need to blush.
He's *John*! Like *Hangs With Hookers!*
Or *Don't forget to flush!*

THREE ABLUTIONARY TALES

1. A Glass of Wine, A Good Hot Bath, and Thou

At times, too sleep-deprived to think
my way from one line to the next
of my next masterpiece, I'll sink
into my bath, to soak, and drink.

Pour me some wine in a nice glass!
It may not, whoops, improve my text
should it by some chance come to pass
I knock it off into the tub,
and lodge its splinters in my ass—

but it's so fine to slurp, and scrub
my boozy body of its stink—
extemporizing, nub by nub,
this Bath Ditty! For thee!
                              Alas,
I dropped my pad and smeared the ink.
Be glad, at least, I do not sext.

2. Your Cachalot: Oh, and Another Thing

And *never* let your cachalot
Join you in the tub.
He only wants to splash a lot,
And his back takes *days* to scrub.

3. Irreconcilable Differences

You prefer to shower;
I prefer to bath—
but not within an hour
of you, you sociopath.

If you'd use just one washcloth—
or move the washcloth rack—
but always *two*—and *dangling* both
to aim their fat, wet flak

down on each side of my brow
in alternating drips!
Why did that bloody marriage vow
ever pass my lips?

How can a union flower
between a wife and hub,
when someone hogs the shower,
and booby traps the tub?

THREE LIMERICKS

1. Apologia to My Pantomime Horse Partner

A pantomime horse may look cute, but
when I play your back half—the suit butt—
it's stuffy, and gloomy,
and rank, and not roomy,
so who gives a hoot it's a cute butt?

2. Underwear

Sometimes, they'll wake, and they'll wonder where
it went. Their lost youth. Their clean underwear.
All that's left in the drawer
is what younger selves wore,
who were fit. When thongs fit. And seemed fun to wear.

3. Memorial Clause for Tandem Paragliders

"Oh Eddie!" she cried, "oh Eduardo!"
as they thrill-rode above Colorado.
Please sign this release
if *you* wish to lease
our equipment, and share their bravado.

COOT

The coot's a glum, derided bird,
who brings her lunch, and sits apart.
She rarely smiles, or says one word,
but nibbles at her apple tart,
and sadly, patiently consumes
the crumbs that dribble down her plumes.
>*Scoot, coot, you bald, fat duck*
>*Your suit's cute, but the tails won't tuck*
>*'Cos your rump's too plump*
>*Like the downtown dump*
>*Scoot, coot, you've got cooties.*

She likes to go for walks, but not
too long a walk, her breath gets short.
She knows she's fat. She's found a spot
behind some reeds, where gnats cavort,
to weigh her shadow on the lake,
and smash its echoes in her wake.
>*Scoot, coot, you old dumb-cluck*
>*Your brain's minute, and your breath's bad luck*
>*You walk wall-eyed! Is there anyone inside?*
>*Hey, babe, you got scabies?*

The water rolling off her back
collects in rills inside her plumes;
the dark beneath of flesh, the black
shut wings, the heart where hardness blooms;
the butt of jokes; the flat, lobed feet.
She dives, and hears the air repeat:
>*Scoot, coot, you big, daft schmuck*
>*Don't hoot, toot, like your car horn's stuck*
>*When your mother took a lover*
>*He was her father and her brother*
>*And their fruit was coot—scoot!*

The coot sits drying in the sun,
and strolls the margin of the lake;
and thinks she might become a nun;
and watches, as she cuts more cake,
the glinting waters whorl and flute;
and dreams of other lives than coot.

THERE ONCE WAS A WINDOW OF LIMBS—

mussed with leaves, in my memory, most times—
    where I watched the wind sport
        with the tenderer parts
of a beech tree that reached me its arms.

I was young, and my heart found delight
in spring dreams. To make love; make light.
    But I studied the law!
        I prepared myself for
life's strictures, its tightening knots.

A professor of torts thissed and thosed.
I half-heard; my eyes rarely closed:
    there were ditties of light,
        and of leafed limbs, I might
have missed, had I yielded and dozed.

There twice was a bird that flew false
and rapped at the room's plate glass walls.
    But just as it knocked,
        I'd looked off, to my book—
or the lectern—anyway, somewhere else—

and was jarred back, but too late to see.
All that stirred were the limbs of my tree,
    unruffled, serene,
        painting all they touched green:
wind-chiming the ruckus from me.

More than three times that age now am I,
and I still love the wind's lullaby
        in the leaves. And am left
    tossed and soothed and bereft
by its spell, in the world's rap and cry.

CHAMELEON METAPHYSICS

Perhaps the world is a mirage
The soul acquires as camouflage?
    He blends into rock,
      And dimly takes stock.

His tongue is long, and quick, and true;
His armor this one trick of hue.
    Not there, he watches.
      What's there, he snatches.

The world, or what he needs of it,
Acquired, subsumed, he feeds off it.
    Not Mephistophelean;
      Merely Chameleon.

MATING SONG OF THE MAYFLY

*'The doliana americana has the shortest lifespan among
species of ephemeroptera; the adult females of the species
live for less than five minutes.... Uniquely among insects,
mayflies possess paired genitalia, with the male having two
aedeagi and the female two gonopores."*
~ Wikipedia

What a life is the mayfly's! Don't scoff:
the adult's sole goal is to boff.
They fly, they lock legs;
as they die, they drop eggs:
pop it in, pop 'em out, and pop off.

And—fun fact—prepare to be wowed—
they come (ahem) doubly endowed.
So they neck and are fecund,
have sex and have seconds
in *seconds*! In hours, they're a crowd.

Thank God our life's more than our phalluses;
that we've time to hurt, heal, and grow calluses;
that we've brains, and willpower!
Still, for one mayfly hour—
nah—I'd need years of analysis.

THE CHAFER AND THE ROSE

What crawls into the rose's maw,
and rubs its darkness softly raw?

How beautiful this rose that gives
its life so that a beetle lives.

How dutiful to its dull ache
this bug that takes for dullness' sake,

beyond all sacramental need
to know or praise, to love or feed,

chafing at its velvet bit
of world until it swallows it.

THE CATBIRD SEAT

The wind is riding his bicycle no hands through
        the corner park—
He is turning wheelies in the grass—
He stands tiptoe from the saddle to tweak the treetops—
Round and round he scampers,
        whistling tunes between his teeth—
And each time he passes the dogwood,
        she waves her pink lace handkerchiefs—
And everywhere he passes, there goes the catbird,
        grey and giddy, riding no hands on his shoulder.

Today, wind-fanned and sunlit, in the corner lot,
I go wading through the buttercups and the forsythia,
Where the crabgrass and the bunched-fist weeds
        rub brown dirt into spring's shazam of gold—

As the catbird wheeling over me
        rides no hands on the shoulder of the wind.

CIMEX, CIMEX: A LOVER'S CURSE
Cimex: the bedbug

Cimex, Cimex, mate upon
the mattress of my ex-friend John,
until he with a grimace sees
a host of little Cimices
crawl between him and his bride
to join them on their buggy ride.
O Cimex, may your stench perfume
the linens of their bridal room.
Where they lie to scratch their itch
inflame the lying dog and bitch
with the nuptial bed bug-bites
of still more carnal appetites—
till limb to limb to limb, you are
their sleepless dark familiar:
yours the name they murmur from
their pitch of shared delirium;
you the succinct ritual oath
sworn faithfully each night by both;
for you their fevered cry at climax:
Bug off, you louse! My thanks, dear Cimex!

(Then since they take your name in vain,
perhaps start right back in again?)

COCKROACHES

Crookshanked skiffs with slicked back wings,
One-inched skulls, jet quick
Couriers of darkness,
Kings of the vanishing trick,
Rustlers in the cupboard's chink,
Outlaw colonials:
All night long I dream you probing
Cracks in my human soul…
Hating, fearing,
Every one,
Such small, quick things I can't control

MARCH OF THE CREEPY-CRAWLIES

(1)

Down the drain, beyond the wall is
The domain of creepy-crawlies.
      At the yard's edge, an alert
      Dung-beetle guards its smudge of dirt.
Plants, and soil, and streams, and creeks
Teem and roil with ants and ticks.
      From the floor joists, just below,
      A feeler foists a tippytoe.
No frontier we gravely draw
Binds one earwig to our law—
      Almost anywhere at all is
      First the lair of creepy-crawlies.

About the thin disputed zone
Of our skin, mosquitos drone—
      Fleas lean in to take our pulse;
      The forelegs preen—the jaws convulse—
From locked drawers, antique wardrobes,
Hardwood floors, emerge microbes—
      Dust mites lurk in a lost wallet—
      Bookworms work their way through Smollett—
Mealy bugs infest the flour—
A longlegs lugs into the shower—
      Cockroaches flock into our kitchen,
      To lick, and poach, antennae twitching.

When I see a silverfish,
All I flee, and all I wish,
      For that stark second, sears my soul—
      And darkness beckons from its hole.

(2)

What's that skitters from us, scattering?
Tiny critters, pitter-pattering.
          In the corner of a crate
Eight-legged fauna fornicate.
In warm earth, fierce cuneiform
          Smears give birth, and swarm, and swarm—
Clothes moths, termites, lice larvae
Rise, go forth, and multiply—
          Till Dow's once best insecticides
          House household spiders' nests inside—
And almost anywhere at all is
First the lair of creepy-crawlies.

(3)

A caked muck's teem, from sleep's once cusp,
Dreams me awake; what hunts, wants us.
In the lawless dark I hear
Creepy-crawlers nudging near.
          A six-legged cricket climbs my nose—
          An eight-legged tick attacks my nose—
A centipede feeds at my breast—
Another twenty knead my chest—
          As if preparing now the terms
          On which they'll share me with the worms.

Where we'll spend our final sleep is
In the land of crawly-creepies.
Thirty feet beneath this rug,
There seethes a silver heat of slugs;
          In that warp and weft of grass
          Two deft scorpions pitpat past—
In the shadows by the gate
Three black widows lie in wait—
          In the attic, or the eaves,
          Something vatic weaves, and weaves.

MY CHICKADEE
for Sally

my little chickadee, sweet little chickadee
parcel of energies, pert and persnickety
would I do this, will I do that
will I still love you when you're old and fat

pale cheeks, a crown that surrounds you with flame
my heart in your mirror repeating your name

soft fluffy flutterer, rising and falling
phone line chit-chatterer, constantly calling
snacker and burrower, lover of naps
nested in hollows of blankets and wraps

dreaming your dreams, of shimmer, and shine
sweet little chickadee, chickadee mine

my little chickadee, sweet little chickadee
dream back our history, Virginia to Picardy
the attic we loved in, the park where we married
the ocean we crossed, this land where we've tarried

on Mulberry Street, in foothills of pine,
sweet little chickadee, chickadee mine

A TORTURED POETRY DEPARTMENT
LIMERICK SUITE
*for Taylor Swift, who timed her release of "The Tortured
Poetry Department" in honor of National Poetry Month*

If only I were Taylor Swift!
Or had that girl's grit, and her gift!
Her minions! her stalkers!
What millions of raucous
and rude tortured limericks I'd shift!

Alas, I'm no scorching hot songstress.
I'm fat in a thong or the wrong dress.
I spit tortured rhymes,
with the wrong stress sometimes,
and I guess they'll do fine (it's the wrong guess).

But today? Hey, Tay fever! Let's catch it!
Midnights? *Folklore*?! Can she match it?
Swifties, my heart!
Let the torture depart!
Go bye-bye, go buy, and go batshit!

TORTURED NPM LIMERICKS, CONTINUED
*Every April (National Poetry Month) for about fifteen years
now, I've drafted new poems daily; most of those years,
I've thrown in a limerick day; sometimes, a limerick or
three are about having a hard time writing daily poems!*

1.
Each April 1st, gallantly, gaily,
I vow to draft new poems daily.
By month's end, each year,
their chime hits my ear
like a forced march for drunk ukulele.

2.
I've not done a whole lot this Easter.
I've mostly just sat on my keister.
Today as I sat,
I thought, "Write about that!"
Cute, huh? Yo soy un artista.

3.
I've been writing—revising—all day.
No new work, though, fit to display.
Some limerick stanzas—
all flatter than Kansas—
like this one. I know! Go away!

TEACHER WORKSONG

With our red pens, our ungraded papers, we are gathered
    to the armchairs & shared workspace of this room
With our bags set in a black dog sprawl about our feet
With a bag here & there with its mouth lolled open,
    with a textbook like a tongue lolled out of it
With our stacks of neat, typed papers: so pretty, still!
    like meditatively boot-tracked lawns of snow
With our tssks & clucks, our red pens' flit of bird-fuss,
    who swoop & flutter & are come to peck
With our silences & punctuating grunts; our pen-squeak
    spattering its blood-trail woe into a slush of margin
With our communal sip-sighs of coffee; our chitchat
    jocularities; our collegial & erudite asides
With now & then an *Aha!* a *Someone-gets-it!* nice fat A!
Then back to spider scribble & footnote screed, to laying
    down the leech-law, to bleeding the error from them

With our classroom whiteboards & our scented markers,
    our great gesticulations & our little jokes
With our rules & their exceptions, our expectations and
    our agendas, here in our little fiefdoms
With our helpfulness, our smiling patience, for you who
    blur before us, back again in your same array of seats
With our faith in you, who know so little, but who have
    come—*again!*—to learn
For really, we've been trying to get the nuances of this
    surely quite straightforward material through your
    skulls for *years* now, for half our clucking life—

With our red pens we are gathered
With our red pens & our patience, our faith & our
    agendas, with our little sighs, our clucks

COCKING A SNOOK

*Aprils when I was teaching full time and had committed to
drafting a new poem daily tired me out. I needed a lot of 10
minute limerick days. Even some 5 minute free verse light
verse days! (Can free verse BE light verse? Pfft, yeah!)
Here's one I like because it's such a slice of that actual life.*

I told my last class of the day that *faire la nique*
    meant *to cock a snook*, forgetting I was talking
    British again and just how hilarious British is;
and also that *faire pfft* meant *to blow a raspberry,*
    which it seemed best to demonstrate;
so that then we spent a good ten minutes
    practicing the rude, rowdy arts of thumbing our nose
    and giving Bronx cheers; until somehow
I found myself adding that *ouah* is *woof,*
    and we wound up barking like a pack of dogs
    pretty much until the bell rang.

And outside the day was so hot—and when I
    got home Sally was out at an evening class—
and inside the house it was just so darn hot—
honestly, it was all I could do to
    dollop up a bowl or two of ice cream
    and fall asleep over a book waiting for her to
get back home, darn it, and give my life meaning again.

Until somehow I was coming to at five to midnight—
    and Sally had long ago left me
    snoring like a pumpkin and gone up to bed.

So! I say.
A five *minute poem, then,* I say.
Ouah!
With a woof and a waggle of my ten fat fingers
    to cock my *pfft* at it as out snooks this.

HUMUHUMUNUKUNUKUAPUA'A

What, then, to me, is the essential quality of light verse? All
poetry *delights in language and in the collision between the
sound and sense of words.* Light verse *gets giddy about it.*

The humuhumunukunukuapua'a swims
The waters of Hawaii with a swish of fishy limbs.
There are many curious aspects to its story I might share,
But only to pronounce its name is something rich & rare:
      humuhumunukunukuapua'a!

It's snout-nosed like a pig, its teeth are sharp and cruel;
It doesn't make great eating, but is good as cooking fuel;
It sleeps wedged in the reef to keep predators at bay;
But all that matters much to me is it's so cool to say:
      humuhumunukunukuapua'a!

It's more than I can handle: some words I *have* to say—
In play, but also prayer, & as much in prayer as play—
For love of incantation, in praise of the collision
Of sibilance, sense, diphthong—glottal, lisp, elision—
To list, to limn, to moan & mean, to mouth, to taste &
      tongue—
In whisper, cry, mixed metrics, to hear them sighed,
      or sung:
Galumph, gallant, galoshes, the Buffster, chuffed,
      chunked, chimp,
Balloon, lagoon, maroon, meringue, harangue, shebang,
      shrimp, blimp,
Chinoiseries, elopement, symbiosis, velcro, flail,
*Harumph, hurrah, hubristic—heptarchical!—*all hail
The dictionary & sea of them! O snook! O tang! O bass!
O fangblenny & sweetlips! O halibut & wrasse!
      O *humuhumunukunukuapua'a!*

JOHNNY & SUSIE'S HALLOWEEN
an audience participation performance piece

It's half past eleven   October 31   the night is as dark
as a black cat in chocolate sauce   & the wind is moaning
like a kettle on a hot plate   & the grown-ups are away
at a Halloween dance   No one is at home   but John &
little Susie   Johnny?   little Susie?   *(long evil laugh)*
All of a sudden   a dog begins to squeal   away in the
distance   like a bad set of brakes   Then two more are
howling   a whole lot closer   like the devil's own
stepkids   tossed out of hell   then four, six, a chorus   of
canine cacophonies   until the walls are quaking   & the
windows are shaking   with the howling, howling of the
dogs *(dog howl)*   Johnny?   little Susie? *(evil laugh)*

REFRAIN: repeat after each stanza, in call & response
Moan, wind, moan   *(WIND MOAN NOISES)*
Howl, dogs, howl   *(DOG HOWL NOISES)*
Thunderclap, clap   *(THUNDER CLAPS)*
Cackle, witch, cackle   *(WITCH CACKLE)*
Scream, kids, scream   *(SCREAMING)*
Tonight is Halloween!
Hallo what? Hallo who? *(all:) HALLOWEEN!*

Now high over the house   come rolls of thunder
like a slag pit collapsing   under scrap heaps of cars
like the sky's a roar of voices   on the rooftops, in the
gutters & they're blubbering at the windows   crying,
Please let me in!   & it's way past their bedtime   but
John & little Susie   are huddled by the TV & they've
turned down the sound   & they're trembling like a
dishwasher   & they're quiet as two houseplants
because someone is knocking at their door   Johnny?
Susie?   someone is knocking at your door *(evil laugh)*

All around the world tonight   witches are walking
disguised as little children   going door to door for treats
& they count up their candy   & if you give 'em craisins
or an apple & a toothbrush   they swell up big as
Disneyworld   & they chug down your TV   yep, you
heard that right!   they just *(chomp noise!)* your TV
Like now, John & Susie!   here at half past spooky!
with it raining bats & bullfrogs!   & somebody
knocking at your door!   Better be ready!   Someone is
knocking at your door! *(evil laugh, cackle, evil laugh)*

Peek through the window   What do you spy?   It's a 4
foot fatty   in a Mickey Mouse mask   she sees you stir
the curtains   she crooks a bony finger: *Come, my little
pretties, let me in!   Come (evil cackle) let me in!*   So
Johnny looks at Susie   & Susie gulps & swallows   &
they sift through their candy   a pretty good haul!   but
not much left   just a thousand chocolate wrappers   &
twenty mucky fingers   & two tummy aches   then the
door creaks open   full of rain & midnight   & a dark,
masked figure   shaking water from a broom   & as she
lifts the mask off her   & she drops it; she enters
Mickey melts in puddles round her shoes *(evil cackle)*

So it's trick or treat for Susie   & it's trick or treat for
Johnny   as the witch asks, "What's for supper?"   &
"YOU ARE" scream the kids   who kill her with karate
cuz she's old & fat & queasy   from eating too much
candy   & gobbling TVs   & gobbling TVs   So now
they watch the late show   they munch on witch &
popcorn   get butter on their night clothes   drop witch
bits in the rug   & the moral of the story?   it's as clear
as chain store windows   never eat the TV!   or never
more than one!   You'll develop indigestion   & be too
fat for karate   Too many TV dinners   are harmful for
your health! *Too many TV dinners wreck your health!*

FOUR *CBEAST* SONG LYRICS

1. Ballad of the Caaing Whale
A name of Scottish origin for the pilot whale, or blackfish

North of the Highlands, north of Kirkwall,
The North Isles of Orkney stand fairest of all.
Where the skerries rise shivering in the froth of the sea,
Where I came with my Jamie, here to North Ronaldsay.
Now it's far by the Shetlands goes the white of his sail,
For he's north among the Faroes, gone to follow
    the caaing whale.

I was born in the Highlands. It was spring in Kirkwall
I met my own Jamie, the fairest of all.
At the kirk of Stennes, there he took me for his bride,
Away to North Ronaldsay rocked me home with the tide.
Now it's far by the Shetlands the white gulls tell his trail,
For he's north among the Faroes, gone to follow
    the caaing whale.

The caaing whale steps to the reel of the waves.
He's led many a poor Orkney man to a cold water grave.
For he'll rise in his thousands, and strike for the deep,
And the price to be paid for his capture is steep.
For he'll frolic through ice fields to jig in the gale,
Far north among the Faroes, singing, "Follow
    the caaing whale."

Now when the wee bairnies who straddle my knee
Have grown into manhood here in North Ronaldsay,
Will they dance like their father to the call of the tide,
And go long from their croft and the arms of their bride?
Far beyond the Shetlands, must they turn and turn tail,
Far north among the Faroes, gone to follow
    the caaing whale?

2. Centaur Drinking Song

My horse's rear is largely torso.
My human front is even more so.
One could not help but be impressed
By my great spaciousness of chest.
Two hearts, four kidneys, twice the liver
Enable me to drink a river.
If only rivers ran retsina,
I'd sleep less thirsty and wake cleaner!

> *With a capacity this big,*
> *It's clear that I was born to swig.*
> *Go in as wine, come out as piddle,*
> *Let's play both ends against the middle—*
> *With a toast to our divine Inventaur,*
> *Who named and made me wholly Centaur.*

Now some may think me a disgrace,
A horse's ass with a human face—
While others marvel, and shape hymns
To praise my six and supple limbs,
My warrior's guile, my strength and speed,
My equine grace, my manly greed.
But sots and singers know me best
For my sheer amplitude of chest.

> *With a capacity this vast,*
> *It's plain I was not born to fast!*
> *So chill the wine, fire up the griddle,*
> *Till meats most meet meet in my middle—*
> *With a toast to our divine Creatyr,*
> *Who neither named nor made me Satyr—*
> *With a toast to our divine Inventaur,*
> *Who named and made us holy Centaur!*

3. Cootie Pageant

Some cooties are beauties, the belles of the ball—
To lice, they're the nicest cooties of all.
Here's to Miss Cootie, 'tis she we salute:
How beauteous her gluteus! Be bounteous, her fruit!

At the Miss Cootie Pageant, held just last night,
Miss Beiruti Cootie & Miss Parisite
Were her Honor Court Cooties! but their queen,
    Ms. Flea's Knees
Was that Cutie of Cooties, Miss Louse Angeles.

Some snooties paraded, & kicked up a ruckus,
And claimed it degraded all decent bloodsuckers—
But how good the loot is! And how grand to see
That Miss Cootie's swimsuit is minuter than she.

Miss Cootie's state duties begin next weekend
With a tour of your city. Please come. Bring a friend!
Singing, "Here's to Miss Cootie, tis she we salute:
How beauteous her gluteus! How hirsute her suit!"

Tonight all the cooties are holding a dance,
They'll party till dawn in the folds of your pants—
And there they will boogie & bop till they drop,
And dance the incomparable Crazed Cootie Hop.

And when they have drunk too much wild dandruff wine
They'll link arms & hiccup in a long cootie line.
That itch that you're feeling around your patootie?
It's maybe the yeehaw of boot-scooting cooties.

Some cooties are goofy, some cooties are gluttons,
Some cooties make whoopee in old folks' belly-buttons,
Some cooties are beauties, the belles of the ball;
And here's to Miss Cootie, the Cutest of All!

4. Chihuahua Blues
Blues and ballads, as song forms (thanks, Trad and Anon!),
exist outside of any light verse tradition, but they can be fun
to use for light verse. Chicago blues is more urban, more
electrified than Delta blues. Chihuahua blues is just sillier.

Got a sweet plump puppy, chihuahua waddle when
       she walk
Got me a sweet plump puppy, she wahwah waddle when
       she walk
There ain't a canine Casanova don't spin round on his
       leash & gawk

She lies on the sofa, chihuahua watches that front door
Just lies on the sofa, she wahwah watches that door
When I walk in through it, she licks my whole face raw

       When she walk, she waddle
       When she lick, she kiss
       When she woof, she holler
       And she howl like this: *[dog wail]*

I let her ride in the front seat, I feed her all the steak
       chihuahua wants
Let her ride in the front seat, let her feed on all the steak
       she wahwah wants
'Cause when I scratch her ears & nuzzle, she just closes
       her big eyes & grunts

I got me a sweet chihuahua, chihuahua warble & wail
I got me a sweet chihuahua, she wahwah warble & wail
She yap she woof she snuffle, chihuahua wag some tail
       (& that's love)

THREE CHALLENGE LIMERICKS

The first of the three is merely in French. The challenge of it is that scansion in French isn't remotely the same as in English. But I wanted to try a French limerick anyway. The second one is a riddle: follow the instructions to solve it—it should rhyme as well as it does in its unsolved riddle form. The third one is actually pretty conventional—once you correct the (counting the title) 16 dyslexic letter shifts!

1. Douche Ditty

Pour le dire en anglais, *he's a douche.*
Face à un joli cul, il y touche.
Si tu cries «Bas les mains!»
il répond «Très bien.
Je me sers plutôt donc de la bouche?»

2. Riddle Limerick

Drop nine leers. The same one. But so
the new word's a word: make though "though";
call sore-bough "sore bough";
he fish "rout" or "trou";
what a he-deer does? "Does on a doe."

3. Dylsexic Great (Straving Artist # 62,433)

In her garter, here's snogwriter Great.
When her big baker comes, file will get better.
Greta rat! Greta sex!
Pulbishers who sing checks!
A Boardway shit how, slick but meat!

A LIMERICK A-Z: Fix the Lost Last Line

*Just for wacky fun, I've moved each last line to the limerick
preceding it, so that Algy now has Zelda's fifth line, Bruce
has pilfered Algy's, Clarence then grabs Bruce's, et cetera.
SHIFT EVERY FIFTH LINE BACK ONE LIMERICK to
repair each poem of the sequence!*

A Decadent poet named Algy
Was subject to fits of *nostalgie*—
Beachcombing the shore
Of his Oceans of Yore,
Until she woke up. Then they belled her.

An underwear model called Bruce,
Being proud of his well-toned caboose,
Had a "shoot the moon" rule:
"You can swoon. You can drool.
In search of laced foam, and lost algae.

"The weight of the blame, though," said Clarence,
"We must lay on my parents' aberrance.
And on theirs, before theirs!
And their forebears' forebears'!
A gander is good. But don't goose."

So biliously soul-dead is Don
He buys his own every con.
Downvote the whole ticket,
Tell his whole mob to stick it,
And…" The court, bored, forbore from forbearance.

An admirer of Jesus called Edith,
Whose vow was to go where He leadeth,
So fought the good fight—
Took the stand for what's right—
And the mob boss will *still* whine he won.

Oh, who is as fickle as Fergus,
Who once, on the night of Walpurgis,
Soul-kissed the Devil,
Then ditched him, mid-revel!
She got handed a Bible to plead with.

A charter boat newbie named Gideon,
Like some bare-torsoed native Floridian,
Steered into the whitecaps,
Swigging drinks meant as nightcaps,
He'd a yen for pre-eucharist burgers.

A grumpy French student named Hortense,
Required to acquire "just one more tense,"
Declared her intention
To—pardon her French—
Till his skin turned less bronze than viridian.

A pair of twins, Evan and Ivan,
Supposing the ploy might enliven
Their dull nine-to-fives,
Switched names, and switched lives.
"Anatomically love word" that poor tense.

A horny old codger named Jeremy
Dreamed dreams of unlived lives more haremy—
As the girl, once, he wed
Surfed Netflix in bed,
And *tried* to switch wives. *One*'s surviving.

A composer for cats, called Katrina,
In *Partita for Spayed Concertina*,
Interweaves hairball wheezes,
Squeezed squeals, and yowled sneezes
To ogle Brad Pitt, and sigh, "Marry me."

Said the prof to the student named Liz,
"If you posit 'It is what it is'—
What *was* 'it'?—or *weren't?*—
Define your referent! "—
Like diseased bees seized by a hyena.

My roommate in college, called Malcolm,
Had odors profusely unwelcome.
How he snored! Like an ox!
Passed out in his jocks
"Will this," she asked, "be on the quiz?"

A Newfoundland nudist named Norman,
Whose log cabin wasn't a warm un,
Regretted, he said,
Being dogless, unwed,
And his socks, while I doused him in talcum.

A gossipy fellow named Otto,
Whose voce was never quite sotto,
Just loved this café!
He could eavesdrop all day,
And preferably a sheik, or a Mormon.

"I landed a mermaid!" said Pedro.
I found this unlikely. I said so.
"I killed, grilled, and ate her,
But puked her up later.
Till we gagged him with force-fed risotto.

Who doesn't love "Crazy Man" Quincy?
The pride of Ohio and Cincy!
What a pro the man is!
Is it all show and biz?
Take a look, dude! She's all in my head, bro!"

A globe-trotting dentist called Ruth
Fell hard for a cannibal youth.
They hungered; they clung;
The auguries swung
Dish the dirt! Where it hurts, and gets chintzy!

As a wizard's apprentice named Sidonie
Was hoovering the spell room, unbidden, the
Demon Lord Black loomed—
She swiveled—she vacuumed—
Between Ruthless and Toothlessly Couth.

Were I the great General Titus,
With foes—and friends—lined up to smite us—
Just where in my slaughter—
Those pies? that raped daughter?—
He got more than he bargained for, didn't he!

Said her host to exchange student Ursula,
"Since the program's designed to immerse you *là*,
On te parle désormais
Uniquement en français.
Might I think, "Will this come back to bite us?"

If you fawn at the feet of Victoria,
She will be unamused, and ignore ya.
But marry King Harry—
Be barren—miscarry—
Ça va, mademoiselle? My, how terse you are!"

A prizefighter nicknamed "Whacks" Wayne,
To mete out the maximum pain,
Would snarl as he smote 'em,
"Yo ma has no scrotum!"
Bear daughters? Your sick transit's gorier.

"Wanna rock tonight," texted Miss X,
"On a tide of below the decks pecks?"
George wrote, "There's a yacht?
With a parrot?" George got
Then they'd scowl, and trade smacks to the brain.

She still had a brain, *tante* Yvonne!
It was mostly just names that were gone.
Her sons'? She was hesitant.
What's yours? Who's the President?
Downrated from triple to ex.

What a cute baby girl was their Zelda!
How she snuffled and purred as they held her!
She slept like a kitten!
They wept! They were smitten!
"*Incroyable!* 'e ran? And Yvonne?"

WARRIOR WORKSONG
after Thomas Love Peacock
parody: *satirical writing that riffs off other creative work;*
pastiche: *writing that does so without satirical intent*

*In a lighter verse collection that wishes to pay homage to
the genre's range—even in as unsystematic a fashion as I
do in* Scattershots—*these twin stratagems are too basic to
the craft not to cite. While "Warrior Worksong" is not the
first piece here I might identify as parody or pastiche, it is
the most blatantly imitative. It cleaves so closely to its anti-
war model, Thomas Love Peacock's "War Song of the
Dinas Vawr" (1829), that it barely crawls out from under
its shadow. And no, it's not funny. Satire, to be effective,
needs primarily to be timely. This topic seems always to be.*

The South has goats and opiates.
The East teems with cheap labor.
We judged it more appropriate
To loot our Northern neighbor.

We marched across the border.
We declared her oilfields ours.
We brought her plains to order.
We leveled a few towers.

Deplored by great committees
Of her ruling fops and fogeys,
We moved in on her cities.
Their bonfires lit our stogies.

Ten thousand palace guards
Girdled the sultan's quarters.
They fell like decks of cards.
We laid claim to his daughters.

Her allies, men of conscience—
Or so they loudly told us
(But what such claims aren't nonsense
In the mouths of rich men's soldiers?)

Rose up to restrain us.
We blew some tanks to pieces.
A blow, it seems, most heinous
When essayed against King Croesus.

Within weeks, they outmanned us.
Our defeat was swift and utter.
They spouted propagandas.
They disgorged us in the gutter.

Now what ticks in their sewers?
Things that scurry, dark and cunning,
With teeth and eyes like skewers?
Count to ten. You're It. Start running.

SEVEN ANSWERS TO THE COOKIE MONSTER CHEER

"The Cookie Monster says that OUR guys are
The great big cookies at the top of the jar

The Cookie Monster says that YOUR guys are
The itty-bitty crumbs at the bottom of the jar"
~a popular high school sports cheer

Well, the Wookie Monster says that you guys cheer
Like a laryngitic Wookie after three kegs of beer

And the Soda Monster says that your team is
An old flat soda without any fizz

And the Pizza monster says that your team's just
Some salvage from the dumpster with bugs in the crust

And the Doughnut Monster says that your team's little
But the hole in some stale glazed peanut brittle

And the Nookie Monster says that your team's merely
A prissy drunken fumble with your fly twice yearly

And the Band Monster says that your team's only
Two tubas in the trunk bumping butts atonally

And the Toilet Monster adds, Keep yanking my chain
And we'll never ever hear from *you* again

CLOUD CUCKOOS

The people in my family
are fools and liars, just like me,
but all of us know how to count,
especially to the wrong amount.
My mother owned a Cuckoo Clock,
kept hidden in her party frock,
that told the time twelve times a year,
until an Angel found it there
and flew her bareback round the sun.
When we turned half of minus one,
he cast her wreckage, fat with us,
under a passing convent bus.

When we were born, the midwife said,
"That twin's ugly. This twin's dead."
My sister gave a banshee shriek.
One almost nun—her heart was weak—
died of shock—I swiped her soul—
and popped right out, alive and whole!
So we went on, as we'd begun,
the Miracle Children, Two and One
(my twin was one and I was too)—
and so, in spurts, we grew and grew,
till she was two and I was three.
But then she grew away from me.
She grew so fast, by half past four
her left arm had to move next door.
She died, of awkwardness, at five:
alone, forgotten, but alive.

Our parents split when I was six.
My mother took to turning tricks.
I learned to curse when I was seven.
Dad said, "You won't go to Heaven."

I shrugged it off, and left, at eight,
for Hollywood, and did so great
we sold the family snake oil mine,
and fished for Cuckoos off Cloud Nine.
There, what wits I'd left, at ten,
I mislaid time and time again—
but bought more cheap, off route 11.
Mom said, "Son, you'll go to Heaven."
Then she and Father hanged themselves,
to lead the way in scuffed size twelves—
just as my long-lost twin of thirteen,
telling the army, "I'm deserting!"
came home to marry me at fourteen!
My parents wept, and started courting!

Life was grand, till she turned fifteen,
lost her job and started drifting,
swigging gin with Windex mixed in,
and left me here with her M16.
When I was saved, and seventeen,
I swore I'd come to Heaven clean,
but man, I got so tired of waiting.
I hitched out, spaceship-style, at eighteen.
Sent this message back at nineteen.
The bottle used to have a pint in,
but I drank it. I was twenty
when the bottle came back empty.

CICADA SONGS

*In praise of all makers of light verse. Part Two is after the
masterful French fabulist Jean de la Fontaine (1621-1695).*

Cicada, littlest hobo,
At dusk, by woodland streams,
Come tune your insect oboe
To ornament my dreams.

Cicada, prince of vagrants,
Along the railroad line,
Shake loose the choral fragrance
From the starlit trumpet vine.

Cicada, inch tall gypsy,
Melt the moonlight in
The singsong of your tipsy
Trembling violin.

I was asleep, and lingering
Where slow winds came and went;
All night, I heard you fingering
A nameless instrument.

Your dew-drenched wings akimbo,
Till dawn, in hoedown pants,
Cicada at my window,
Reteach my soul its dance.

Cicada, who had spent his summer singing,
down where the hickories and hemlocks bent
over their slow reflections in the creek,
looked up to find the weather had turned bleak;
that ground-frosts clinging to the grass had pent
his little world in mortuary stone.
And found he was near naked, and half-starved.

To Cousin Ant he flew, our Foreman-King, who carved
this our Empire from the dirt, to squeeze us for a loan.
"Or work!" he chirped, as through Queen's Wood
November winds blew, measuring the seams
of shadows, and the world for snow.
Our Cousin looked him over with a smirk.
"What work, pipsqueak?" Ten thousand ants
seethed round, intent on schemes
such as Cicada haven't the wits to know.
"I can sing! Like a bird! All night! I'm good."
"So I've heard," Ant sighed. "All right. I fear
we have no grants for whistlers in the dark this year,
but do you dance? I'm told the starved bard hop
staves off the cold and curbs the appetite."
But even as we turned our snickering backs,
"Yeehaw!" he cried, and hitching up his pants,
high-kicking his six limbs, began to bop.

I learned this tale from Ant, our Foreman-King,
who colored it a strange and glorious thing—
the foolish dancer; his foot-flailing dance;
the ribald laughter of ten thousand ants;
the beat he kept time by we strained to hear.
We named him our Court Clown, and fed him leaf;
and yet, at morning light, they found him gone.

But sometimes since, we catch a shifting tone
of wind in trees, by creeks and railroad tracks—
a whisper far away—the spondee moan
train whistles make, before the shunt of cars—
and pause, unnerved, antennae trembling;
and cannot tell what moves us, joy or grief.
Some say it is the song cicadas sing,
performing to their audience of stars.

ACKNOWLEDGMENTS: a big thank you to the publications where a few of these pieces first appeared:

"Corgis and Bess" in Light, whose editors nominated it
        for a Pushcart Prize and for Best of the Net
"Dangerous Liaisons" in *A Betabestiary*
"The Art of the Limerick" in Poetry Virginia
"Lament over the Lack of Ham" in *The Hamthology*
"Cat, Cat" in the *WAM Animals Anthology*
"Political Damp Squib #1" in Rigorous
(Others appeared briefly in contest awards brochures; or on an art gallery wall; or have been featured, in some form, on my website, www.petalridge.com.)

How all over the place is Mr. Kannemeyer!
A slut for about every paradigm!
He waltzes from schmaltz to verbal assaults
of sheer silliness, subtle as cannon fire.
He lightly delights, then expounds, then he scoffs,
lets the textures compound, into rattling coughs
that he hacks up in hairballs of rhyme.
(And what's with those prefatory lectures?)
But he's had him a rattling fun time;
and he hopes some of it was infectious.